Epigenetic Sonnets

Graham Everett

ISBN: 978-93-6354-432-1

First Edition: 2024
Rs. 200/-

Cyberwit.net
HIG 45 Kaushambi Kunj, Kalindipuram
Allahabad - 211011 (U.P.) India
http://www.cyberwit.net
Tel: +(91) 9415091004
E-mail: info@cyberwit.net

Printed at Repro India Limited.

Dedicated to Elyse, Logan and Ali

Credits for previously published poems:

"Ain't Every Day Wonderful," "Neither Politics Nor Religion," and "Muse Bait" first appeared *in Long Island Sounds: 2023*. Edited by Tammy Nuzzo-Morgan, Robert Savino, and Billy Hands. The North Sea Poetry Scene Press, NY.

"Standing Under the Sky" first appeared in *Poetry Bay* by Long Island Quarterly, Winter 2022-2023.

Collections of Poetry

Ocean, Clouds, Life (private, 1969).

Sources of Hope (private, 1972).

Casting Bones from a Turtle Shell: Street Press, 1977.

Rural Gardenia: TK Press, 1977.

Nothing Left to Fake: A Great American 4 Page Novel: The Black Hole School of Poethnics, 1978.

The Trees. Port Jefferson, N.Y.: Street Press, 1978

Strange Coast. Potsdam, N.Y.: Tamarack Editions, 1979

Nightlights and Crickets (private, 1983).

The Sunlit Sidewalk. Syracuse, N.Y.: Tamarack Editions, 1985.

Minus Green. New Hampton, N.Y.: Yank This Press, 1992.

Minus Green Plus. Sound Beach, N.Y.: Breeze/Street Press, 1995.

The Doc Fayth Poems: Street/Mongrel, 1998.

Corps Calleux: Street, 2000.

That Nod Toward Love: New Poems: Street Press, 2006.

An Incomplete Dictionary of Disappearing Things: Street, 2012

Living with Others: Street Press, 2015

Broadsides

Trees. Mastic, N.Y.: Street Press, 1976

Farewell to the Decade & Liberty Avenue. Port Jefferson [NY]: Black Hole School of Poethnics, 1980.

Letter to Everywoman. Potsdam, N.Y.: Banjo Press, 1978.

This Could Be Plutonium: Ukulele Press, 1978.

Winding the Alarm Clock. Potsdam, N.Y.: Banjo Press, 1979.

Facing 1984 (private, 1984).

Published poems by Graham Everett

1970: "In the Common," and "The Doubting Sanctuary" in *Paradox 7*, Winter-Spring 1970 (p. 18).

1974: "Shaman's Chuckle," and "Some Examples of Our Oneness" in *Empty Belly* #3, 1974.

1975: "Near the Route Home," "Under a Full Moon" in *Bird Effort*, Issue 1-2, 1975 (p. 22). "Hunter Visions on the Beach," and "Exercise" in *East End Anthology*, 1975.

"Cornucopia" in *Mr. Cogito*, Volume 1, Number 3, 1975.

1976: "An Assay," and "Long After" in *Grub Street: A Collection of Verse Fiction and Graphics,* No. 5, 1976 (p. 20). "The Earth Warms Quickly in Spring" in *Mojo Navigator(e)* #5, 1976 (p. 8). "Jazz" in *The Voyeur,* Volume 2, No. 8, August 1976 (p.8). "Between Beers Buddhism" in *The Voyeur*, Volume 2, No, 9, September 1976 (p. 3). "Poem Seven," in *The Voyeur*, Volume 2, No. 10, October 1976 (p. 7).

1977: "Between Beers Buddhism," Anarchy," "Landless And" in *Bird Effort*, Issue 3-4 (For John Hall Wheelock), 1977 (pp. 22-23). "Standing this Land" in *Wetlands*, Volume 5, Number 4, Winter 1977 (p. 28).

1978: "Sidestep," and "For Elyse" in *Risings: An Anthology*, 1978 (p. 16).

1979: "Wrestling with the Muse," in *Gravida* 16, 1979 (p. 5). "Claro" in *San Fernando Poetry Journal*, Vol. 3, No. 3, 1979 p.28). "Reprieve in Taos," and "Borderline Nightmare" in *Scree* 11-12, Native American Issue 1979 (p. 29). "Letter to Everywoman," "Walking in What Were Once Woods," These Trees are Happy with the Rain," "To Talk with the Tree People," and "Night Vision" in *Tamarack*, Issue 2, Spring-Summer 1979 (pp.14-18). "The Potbelly Stove" in *The Walrus Said*, Volume 11, August 27, 1979 (p. 10).

1980: "No More," and "By The Side of the Road: 1968" in *Intrepid: Bill Williams and Flossie's Special*, 39-40, 1980 (edited by Allen DeLoach) (pp. 93-94). Questions" in *West Hills Review: A Walt Whitman Journal*, Volume Two, Fall 1980 (p. 89). "Music" in *Zephyr*, Volume 1, Issue 1, 1980 (p. 9).

1981: "The Pot-bellied Stove" in *On Good Ground: Poems and Photographs of Eastern Long Island*. Edited by Ray Freed and Jim Tyack. NY: Street Press, 1981.

1982: "Sand on the Sidewalk," in Poets and Artists, 1982 (p. 9). "Winding the Alarm Clock" in *Zephyr*, Volume 2, Issue 1, 1982 (p. 7). "Thirteen, Full of Life" in *Wetting Our Lines Together: An Anthology of Recent North American Fishing Poems*. Edited by Allen Hoey. NY: Tamarack Press, 1982.

1983: "The Eastern Butterfly," and "Night Returns Winter" in *Bluefish*, V.1, #1, Autumn 1983 (pp. 58-59). "Reincarnation is Boring" in *The Cathartic*, Spring 1983 (p. 4). "MO." in *Dead Angel* 4, Volume 1, Number 4, 1983 (p. 16). Exorcism" in *Earth's Daughters,* 19-20. 1983 (p. 27). "Who Doesn't Expect Something" in *Laughing Bear, Poetry Series No. 1*, 1983. "Vitality is Variety in Unity" *Writings from the Mills Pond House:1983.* (p. 5-6). "The Cows are Chewing Their Barns to Pieces," "Crickets in February," "Evacuate" in *Rabid Chalk*, edited by M. Costello (pp. 18-20).

1984: *Literary Assays* by Allen DeLoach (1984) (Graham and Elyse Everett: "The Frog and Oriental Princess," postcard). "In the Middle is a Dream" in *Zephyr*, Volume 2, Issue 2, 1984 (p. 19).

1985: "And Now I've Done My Part," and "Autumn Refractive" in *Bluefish*, V.2, #3/4, Autumn 84/Spring 85 (p. 137). "Ritual" in *Creations on Creation: A Chapbook of Nature Poetry* edited by Tom Stock, 1985 (p. 7).

1986: "Crime," "Driving," and "Having a Vision" in *Riverrun*, Spring 1986 (pp. 14, 19, 94). "Pulling the Days Together," "Early May," "Day/

Night," "Near hanksgiving," "January," "Families at the Shore,"and "Here"in *Long Island Poets*. Edited by Robert Long. NY: The Permanent Press, 1986.

1987: "So Long" in *Bluefish*, V.3, #5/6, Spring/Summer 1987 (p. 79). "Dead Lines" in *Brook Spring*, 1987 (p. 20). "Latest Victim" in *Cabaret*, Volume One, Number One, 1987. "Often"(for Logan), "August Twenty-First," "The Spread of My Body" *Podium*, V. VI, April 1987 (p. 19). "Dear Reader" in *Slow Motion Magazine*, Issue 3, Spring 1987 (p. 32).

1988: "Crickets in February" in *Brook Spring*, 1988 (p. 7). "Owed to Fate," in *Redstart,* Vol. 2, Issue 1, 1988 (p. 54).

1989: "Break Out the Down" in *Caprice*, April 1989 (p. 33). "Among the Scrub Oak and Windblown Silt" in *Scrub Oak Review: The Literary Magazine of Southampton College*, 1989.

1990: "Worldly" in *Brook Spring*, 1990 (p. 6). "Minus Green" in *Long Island Quarterly*, Spring, 1990. "The Colors This Spring" in *Long Island Quarterly*, Summer, 1990. Introduction to *Smoke Stack: A Collection of New Poetry*, 1990.

1991: "The 92-Year-Old-Man" in *Caprice*, February, 1991 (p. 54). "Here" in *Live Poets*, Volume 1, Issue 1, 1991 (p. 19). "Summer, Sunday Night" in *Long Island Quarterly,* Autumn 1991. "Daily Rounds" in *Voices of the Vine*, Summer 1991.

1992: "Near Thanksgiving" in *Contact/II: A Poetry Review*, Spring 1992 (p. 55). "New World Order" in *Live Poets*, Volume 1, Issue 2, 1992 (p. 89). "Estate" in *Scrub Oak Review*: *The Literary Magazine of Southampton College*, 1992 (p. 34).

1993: "Eve of March Seventh," Against The Powers That Be," "Outside Bohemia," and "Along Route 25A" in *4X4*, Fall, 1993. "Two-Car Marriage" in *Caprice*, March 1993 (p. 38).

1994: *Poems for David Ignatow.* Edited by Robert Long. NY: Canio's Editions, 1994.

In Autumn. Edited by George Wallace. NY: Birnham Wood Graphics, 1994.

1996: "In Reply" in *Caprice*, January 1996 (p. 13). "The Colors This Spring"in *Dumb Beautiful Ministers*. Selected by William Heyen. NY: Birnham Wood Graphics, 1996.

1997: "Breaking Quiet Desperation" in *Asinine Poetry*, Numero Uno, Spring 1997.

1998: "That Close" in *Asinine Poetry*, Issue No. 2, Spring 1998. "Break Out the Down" in *Cocodrilo*, Vol. I., No.1, Fall 1998. "High KU" in *Asinine Poetry*, Issue No. 5, Summer 1998.

1999: "Breaking Quiet Desperation" reprinted in *Asinine Poetry: Collectors' Edition*, Spring 1999.

[Any explanation for hiatus?]

2005: "Harvesting Flesh," and "The Future" in *Mind Gorilla*, Volume 1, Issue No. 9, December 2005 (p. 4). "Tacit No More," "Human History," and "Mostly" in Long Island Sounds, 2005: *An Anthology of Poetry from Maspeth to Montauk*. Edited by Tammy Nuzzo-Morgan and Gail Koop. NY: The North Sea Poetry Scene Press, 2005. "It Was Some Night," and "Orpheus in Squirrel Stance" in *Asinine Love Poetry*. NY: AsininePoetry.com, 2005.

2006: "Early Thaw," "Resolutions," "So Much for Human Desire," and "Winter's Discontent," in *Long Island Sounds 2006: An Anthology of Poetry from Maspeth to Montauk and Beyond* (pp. 55-56). "An Elegy Toward Happiness," "This Started Out Being About You," and "Last Two Weeks Before Summer" in *The Light of City and Sea: An Anthology of Suffolk County Poetry*. Edited by Daniel Thomas Moran et al. Street Press, 2006.

2007: "Old Truths" in Swansea Poetry Magazine, Issue Six. Summer, 2007 (p. 40). "3 Post Cards," "Breaking Pattern," "Honu," "Sonata," and “The Task” in *LongIsland Sounds 2007: An Anthology of Poetry from Maspeth to Montauk and Beyond.* Edited by Tammy Nuzzo-Morgan et al. (pp. 99-103).

2008: “Latest Victim” in *The Lineup: Poems on Crime*. Edited by Gerald So, et al. (p. 7).

“Full Circle,” “Bonus Time,” and “A Hackneyed Yet Gentle Reminder” in *Long Island Sounds 2008: An Anthology of Poetry from Maspeth to Montauk and Beyond.* Edited by Tammy Nuzzo-Morgan et al. (pp. 289-291).

2009: 14 poems in *Paumanok/Long Island: Poems and Pictures*. Edited by Kathaleen Donnely. “A Zendo Date with Elizabeth Satori,” and “Sayonara” in *Writing Outside the Lines.* Edited by Tammy Nuzzo-Morgan and Peter V. Dugan. Wild Side Press, 2009.

Published Articles

“A Reading of Walt Whitman’s ‘Give Me The Splendid Silent Sun,’” in *West Hills Review: A Walt Whitman Journal*, Volume Eight, 1988 (pp. 105-111)

“Yes, How Strange Life’s Venture: Comments on John Hall Wheelock’s Dear Men and Women.” *North Atlantic Review*, 1990.

“Emerging Meaning: Reading as a Process.” *Teaching in the 21st Century.* Alice Robertson and Barbara Smith, Eds. NY: Falmer Press, 1999.

Co-edited Published Anthologies

Paumanok Rising: An Anthology of Eastern Long Island Aesthetics. Edited by Vince Clemente and Graham Everett. NY: Street Press, 1982.

Writing Workshop Anthology No. 1. Edited by Allen Planz and Graham Everett. Backstreet Editions, 1982.

The Light of City and Sea: An Anthology of Suffolk County Poetry. Edited by Daniel Thomas Moran et al. Street Press, 2006.

Books Published by Graham Everett - Street Press

Necessary Lies, Ray Freed
Short Circuits, Dan Murray
Street of Lost Fools, Jack Micheline
Rented Tuxedo, Jim Tyack
Laurie's Songs, R.B. Weber
Release The Breathless, Bonnie Gordon
Sea Story, C.B. Fleming
Here & There, Claire Nicolas White
Shinnecock Bay, Ray Freed
Trees, Graham Everett
Poems From The Island, Jonathan Cohen
Dead Reckoning, Ron Overton
Locating Positions, Joy Walsh
Moom, Ray Freed
Arriving on Paumanok, Norbert Krapf
Village Vignettes, Michael Braude
Cedar Light, Allen Hoey
She, Lucille Quinitchette
Chunderhara, Allen Planz
Getting Out of Town, Robert Long
From This Book of Praise, Vince Clemente
Poems From The Xenia Hotel, R.B. Weber
In Chontales, Richard Elman
Just As The Boy Dreams…, Michelle Cusumano
Casting Bones From A Turtle Shell, Graham Everett
Paumanok Rising, Eds.,Vince Clemente and Graham Everett

On Good Ground, Eds, Ray Freed and Jim Tyack
Shinneck Bay & Boston Poems, Homer Lawrence
What It Is, Robert Long
Childhood In Reno, Bonnie Gordon
Surf Club, Edward Harsen
The Fishing-Print Poems, R.B. Weber
Lightouch, Bud Navero
My 187th Birthday Party, Michael Braude
Much Cry, Little Wool, Ray Freed
Endless Staircase, Sandy McIntosh
Hulalali Poems, Ray Freed
Limousine To Nowhere, Jim Tyack
None of This Is On The Map, Dan Murray
Minus Green Plus, Graham Everett
Fandango, Marge Miller
On Boca Ciega Bay, Thomas Duddy
Pat Sonnets, Max Wickert
All Horses Are Flowers, Ray Freed
The Doc Fayth Poems, Ed., Graham Everett
Corps Calleux, Graham Everett
Regarding The Snow, Thomas Duddy
From Willow Pond to Hilo, Daniel Thomas Moran
Brooklyn Born, Lenny Greco
World Trade Center Poems, Fred Byrnes
The Bitter & The Sweet, Tammy Nuzzo-Morgan
The Light of City and Sea, Eds., Daniel Thomas Moran et al.
Let Me Tell You Something, Tammy Nuzzo-Morgan
That Nod Toward Love, Graham Everett
Part Mirth, Part Murder, Dan Giancola
Artifacts of Sound, Annabelle Moseley
Creaturely Drift, Allen Planz
Still Life, Annabelle Moseley
Stopping In Front of The Chelsea, Fred Byrnes

The Delaney, Annabelle Moseley
Sicilian Rhapsody, Leonard Greco
Silver Fish, Ray Freed
The Space Between, George Dorsty
Data Error, Dan Giancola
An Incomplete Dictionary of Disappearing Things, Graham Everett
Living with Others, Graham Everett

Publisher and Editor-in-Chief of *Street Magazine*
Volume One
Issue One: Premier Issue (1972?)
Issue Two; Kids' Poems
Issue Three: American Politics/Male & Female (artwork by Van Howell)
Issue Four: Kerouac
Volume Two
Issue One: Long Island Issue
Issue Two: Collage/Workshop Poetry Issue, Guest Editor: R.B. Weber Issue Three: South American Poetry Issue, Guest Editor: Jonathan Cohen
Issue Four: Beat/Energy

Volume Three
Issue One
Issue Two: Humor/Parody Issue, Guest Editor: Jim Tyack
Issue Three: Woman's Issue, Guest Editor: Claire Nicolas White
Issue Four – unpublished

Digital Issues
1, Spring/Summer 2007
2, Autumn 2007
3, Summer 2008

4, Winter 2008-2009
5, Winter 2010-2011
6, Summer 2011
7,
8,
9, Autumn 2013

Artist at Work Series: Digital Documentaries on artists, focusing on each featured artist's education, art, and artistic process.

Michael Calabrese, Abstract Expressionist
Graham Everett, Constructionist
Jim Tyack, Artist
Robert White: The Body Electric, Sculptor
Janene Gentile, Expressionist
Jack Graves III, Artist
Brian Mullahy, Woodworker
Ray Freed, Poet

Contents

The poems in *Epigenetic Sonnets* are classic Everett poems and they have the odd effect of making me feel I am sitting and listening to him tell his stories. He is unique in my experience in that his poems are so much like a diary and a meditation. There are also a lot of great lines along the way. I have never written as I suspect he might write. I can go weeks and not write anything resembling a poem but then insight hits and I write. Everett's poems are more a recording of time as it passes with each day having something to write about and that gives the poems a quiet, understated beauty.

— Daniel Thomas Moran, 2024

Acknowledgements

With deep thanks and respect to friends and poets who provided feedback as these poems evolved. They offered their useful editing and poetic advice:

Jon Cohen, Dan Giancola, Daniel Thomas Moran,

Richie Narvaez, Tom Stock, and forgotten others.

Ain't Every Day Wonderful

When tough turns to rough and it's cold
and your toes get feeling tingly
you think of warm days at the beach

You can manage that mindless mindset
when you reset, make that happen

Ain't every day wonderful
Ain't every day wonderful

New rugs by the rainy day doors
New strains on drug store shelves

Taking it all real slow when the sunshine
slanting in, streams through open blinds

Digging all human history
Survive and flourish

Ain't every day wonderful

An Account

I'm riding my bike falling after trying to turn too quick
that moment when balance goes off and a tuck and roll
leaves the right knee and edge of the helmet to hit the road

Look around, make sure no cars are coming, and get up
Checking damage to me and the bike as I get back on
and slow ride the short way home. Ice pack, bandages

Recollecting the other incidents and injuries
slight as they've been, as lucky as I've been – well
aware of the inches away from death each time

Side of my head must've kissed the asphalt. Glad I wore
a helmet – wished I'd had another one for my knee

Later, mulling how many accidents happen every day
No need to rile anyone up, enough bad stuff going on

After a while many scars lose their stories

An Ordered Life

Rain meets the forecast – right on time: 4:00 pm
No wind, just hot and humid, so you can hear
the rain drops come down through the trees
splashing them leaves, dancing the rim
of a water can keeping time with a steady beat

Fix dinner, eat dinner, clean up after dinner
Go to sleep. Wake up. Fix breakfast, eat, drink
coffee. Sit around doing puzzles till near noon

Spouse and I take a trash can each. The re-
cycle can gets three feet from the other daily
garbage: kitchen, bath, and various projects

The gathering of the kibble, the packaging
Who knows where it all goes – off into space
between 9:30 and 11:00 tomorrow morning

Announced and Delayed

I ate more potato chips than recommended
Smoked, drank, had lax personal habits, and
stayed in a local limelight until bored
I left looking to be a nobody, thank you

The others had their reasons for wanting out
or staying there. All fine with me – hydrating
and finding a cool neighborhood to live in

Dinner over. Dishes done. Dog's been out
Time to relax, kick back and try not
to get all caught up in the ways things were
or even are – it's all one, then nothing
then bits of everything forgetting how to fit

The music circles back around. Any ghosts
left pose no threat. Believe me! Back in a bit

Beasts

A tad below freezing last night
and the cold lingers, then jumps to fifty
Near noon it's almost fit to do the chores

Another day gone but not without the dog
catching a squirrel and me running around
telling the dog to drop it, and then sit – enough
to pick the dog up and bring it inside

I go back out with a flashlight to help
the squirrel, its back legs limp
drag itself into a safe spot among rocks

I don't have the heart to just kill it
though that might be the merciful thing to do

Now a matter of keeping the dog in till I can
get back out there and discard its corpse

Climbing that Hill

Wish I knew what put him over the line
calling for names and alliances at the slightest
hint of disloyalty. He could have been an artist
demanding everyone get a good collage education

The con quips his jokes that work for most incidences
Some fear him as a mind bender. Many worship him
for exactly that power – Make the world the way we
want it to be! Must find out whom "we" includes

Usually a hard to describe endeavor where failing
to lash himself to the mast, the captain goes mad

Ahab dragged into the sea, his harpoon hard set
          in the stricken side of the escaping white whale

That unfathomable sea – Ahab bouncing in those waves
like a body dragged over rock and gully up that very hill

Darn, Darn, Darn

Woke this morning to things falling apart
and went back to sleep for an hour or two
or at least I intended to do that but was told
get up and fix breakfast, damn it. "No rest
for the weary" floats through that mental
landscape, the mind's expanse the color
of a blind eye clouded, opaline, yet those
who might care are no longer here. "Poo-

tee-weet" and "So it goes" haven't changed
If one leaves the past behind, will it show up
again, even when one has little need for it?

One too many question gimp a resolution
That's probably for you the reader to offer
Speak, someone out there may hear you

Domestic Issue

The new countertops are lower than the old ones
by about an inch – just enough to make us feel taller
The sink is bigger, the quartz glitters, sparkles

Remembering where everything goes is a challenge
best dealt with by the moving process of elimination

The plumber was here this morning bending pipes
to accommodate two drains into one. The dishwasher
drains out the one capped off. The kitchen is back!

Getting the fourth of our living spaces to be comfortable
is almost easier than the previous two. The second one
we had little money but a lot of sweat equity. This one

well bank-rolled, has a few more projects to do. Then
we'll sit back and enjoy the view: the trees, the blue sky
stretching into night, the stars playing good-time music

Freedom – Responsibility = Chaos

This used to be the season of joy and goodwill
Now it's become the time all the crazies spout
their unsocial rants not based in reality

I can't write letters to Congress 'cause my words
may sound as angry and crazed as the crazies' rants
It's tough to deal sanely with such irrationality
especially with those who yearn to scuttle the law

There's close to 40 percent of this country's voters
who display not more than a 6th-grade reading level
Informed by base bigotry and weird idolatry
they run rampant these days beyond clear control

Our previous fears of a conman helming the state ship
prove to be true. The problem now is not easy to right
Perhaps valid redefinitions of country and citizenry might

Gin Joint Etude

So I say to the characters in the Bard's plays
Today we'd speak those lines this way, at times
There're many ways to say the lines in any play

Away, no more bending my ear, having words
that stride no more the roads of clarity
instead roam the alleys of ambiguity
    once again. How droll

A generation coming of age ex post millennium
has said it, and will soon enough be looking
to be roaring in their twenties – don't be late

Been hanging on the edge, minding my own
Reading some books, listening to the radio
            Nighttime is well on its way
    Peace will rule

Got Lots to Do

A couple of hours a day spackling and taping
the studio walls – my skills at such getting honed
as I proceed. It's not a living room – it'll be nice
enough. I'll be glad when the task is finished

The venues in this town keep crazy hours
A local nursery closes on Wednesdays
A great place for Pho soup closes on Mondays
Getting to be where it pays to call ahead

Made one of my favorite dinners and dined well
Ready soon to shake a batch of Sidecar cocktails

One more cold night below freezing, then
a warming spell for first weekend in December
The pendulum tending toward winter solstice
Another turn around the sun for all of us

Growing Old, Shrinking

Some nomads leave valuable things behind: living
room furniture; makeshift bookcases; cookware
– woks, fondue pots; a cherished pea coat; and
various singed notebooks. The places were real
The events well lived. So each traveler attests

Easily tired, this old guy paces his steps and bends
to pull weeds, snip unwanted tree sprouts in the rock
garden covered in *vinca*, periwinkle flowers gone

He sits on the deck rejuvenating his energy
Ready soon to continue his gardening tasks

Gazing at bumble bees gathering nectar
      from the first bursts of crocus
                  their buzzing resonates with
Earth in sunshine warmth, he sighs and smiles

I Got My Own Conspiracies

The nameless one emanates the satire side of Machiavelli
weighs-in when it benefits his mood. People fall for his act
that's what really worries me more than the comet heading
toward earth, or the Stock Market crash, or that thin ruse
of banning books – a mere distraction from the arms deals

Once again we're in the world of being against laws, social
ethics, science, and most change. Everybody has an opinion
and many of them are exactly alike – majority rule without
empathy is empty neighborhoods, bankrupt enterprises
angry kids, all those social evils that keep coming round

like silly votes that say a church can only feed the hungry
two nights a week, no water for voters waiting on line
Those behind this mess want to rule the world, all the money
in their pockets, hire bruisers to provide security. Shit

I Used to Pray Now I Write

May all gods turn out strong and mindful
merciful and understanding of humankind

The mistakes made that hobble me still, the killings
around the world according to today's news
the lovers betrayed, the followers misled
the carelessness of doing what you got to do

To live free of hate is not easy. To keep at it
is difficult – but there is more yet to be done

Trouble keeps occurring. We get better at see-
ing it coming, limiting the damage, and
quickening the clean up. Getting back
to normal quickly is the new norm

But that is not enough – we have to get
at the dark heart of humanity and love it

In My View

A lot of people I've known know next to nothing
about religion, politics, or science. They barely
know what they know. Not that they're idiots
But they either lack or don't use critical thinking

And what's worse they seem to ignore
any but their own freedom. They eschew
empathy – so sure who the enemy is and what
those opposed to them think or plan to do

A polarization with which I refuse to take sides
Each day a new wonder arises, not always
an immense one, but intriguing enough
that I'm caught by it – in the grasp of beauty

Friendships that die today, for whatever reasons
get file-boxed under "Past" in a large storage room

Kicks

Sometimes you can tell when someone is lying to you
Most of the time you can't with any surety or evidence
So it's a matter of trust. You live with the lie. You learn

to play along with the words and the chords, a song
But what you learn does not last forever
That muscle memory fades, easily forgotten

More rain falling, thin, steady. Lucky to total
half an inch. Though badly needed. Around here
any temps below fifty degrees gets deemed cold

Now the row of holidays and diverse cultures
celebrating this natural occurrence. Let them
Searches for truth can turn endless, mostly empty

On the bright side we made it to the Winter Solstice
Let the slow return of light and re-warming begin

Lineage

Two bright male cardinals fight
Not much has changed
One hears the rain blowing in

We can only be ourselves
being whomever we want
So live and die happy or not

A couple of jabs and one stops worrying
about the virus, silly tyrants, and
the world beyond this forest in spring

The wind rises, uplifting boughs
in its quick path crows caw cawing
A smell of rain on this incoming motion

All goes quiet. A few minutes fade
into a sort of silence one can hear

Maintaining Balance

Yesterday I woke from dreaming fried eggs for breakfast
This morning I want to get out and do yard work, stretch
Gathering the tree fall in the yard waste bin I move my body
It's evening now and my legs, arms, and back ache nicely

The list of things to do to maintain and upgrade this house
grows shorter but is still expensive: sealing the crawlspace
fixing the electrical hookup, putting in a new fuse panel box
trimming the trees, replacing the garage door on the studio

And down the road a good repair of the cracked driveway
Its concrete-like Tectonic-plates need fixing, reshifting
Angles too dangerous for tires and our walking feet

A couple of tokes of ground sativa bud help me to relax
There's a slow rain falling outside muffled by pine
needles on the metal roof. A soft music, an easy exhale

Meandering

Woken at 4:30 a.m. by a barrage of thunder
I'm barely able to slip back into sleep
The wind blows the rain against the house
The rain turns to sleet and snow
A dusting covers the lawns and streets

Early afternoon the sun comes out
Melts the snow and dries the mud
The rest of today goes by in a haze

Now the sky is dark as night again
Dinner is eaten in several sittings
Just enough to fill the hunger pit

Time to set a list of people to write to
A list of needed things to see if I can find
as I familiarize my car with these new roads

Moments of Clarity

A profusion of mushrooms obviously triggered
by the recent solar flare that lashed Earth. There's only
been a little rain in the past few weeks – hardly enough
to cause such blossom and diversity: Death Angels
Amanitas, yellow ones like coral, abnormally huge
ones in various shades of whites, browns and greys

Perhaps such otherworldly spinning occurs silently
like crossing four lanes of never mind the speed limit

Tomorrow I enter three to four nights of living alone
A trial hermitage, a prep for being on one's own

Right now, the TV goes on to placate the dog
that wants spouse and I to come sit with it
                    marking the evening into the night

Don't promise anything, just show up

Mont Sainte-Victorie in Part

Cezanne painted the same mountain many times
Was he searching for the essence of that mountain
or simply recording how it was always changing?

No doubt, I know more about mountains
than I know Cezanne, and more about mountains
than I remember about the saints – yet they both
change in the passing arch of sunlight or looking
at them from afar, majestic, unscalable. Yet closer
and even driving or hiking up hills there're more
quite similar, others much different – not like saints

Riding from Taos to Denver through the Rockies
I saw many types of rainbows – concentric, leaping
extra brilliant in that high thin air. My face pressed
to the bus window as if I were riding on the moon

Mortality

It’s been said that the good die young, others keep aging
Begin to experience the swift loss of a line of thought
It’s harder now to think things through in the mind. Back
to writing ideas and plans down like a grocery list, like
putting together a jigsaw puzzle without the picture
to stay the fear of chaos and all the loses that entails

Stand clear, it’s time to switch topics and stay cool
Who knows when the alarms might next sound
More snow forecast overnight and into tomorrow
Yet we’re further enough south that it will melt
before too many days go by. Yet time won’t heal
the lovers and beautiful ones gone away too soon

How much energy to keep on counterbalances
with how much real work one gets done before dying

Muse Bait

No idea if this path leads to the river
I listen for the gurgling drift of babbling water
One step leads to the next with time to stop
and determine if the sounds get louder or softer
I want to know if I am getting closer or farther away
The walk down makes sense geographically
Most rivers create valleys in the land they run thru
My aim is to paint with words these scenes of beauty
When I come to the river I will walk its meanders
rather than gauge its depth or dare to cross it
I might sit and watch it flow getting all philosophical
guessing the hidden meanings in sticks and rocks
Simply sitting, not even waiting to see what floats by
Simply listening without putting words to the sounds

Hole in the Roof

I don’t want you to mess with him
You know he was once a gunman

I just want this one dance with you
— I’m not looking for a lifetime

Stand up mamma, tell me want you want
I got fifty dollars in my back pocket

Felt like a big boy downtown all by myself
Didn’t find the bookstore, but I found Pho

Wasn’t driving the car with a package to send
I’m sure I’ll be back in this part of town again

Trying out some bud a friend had grown
Gentle choking — heaven bent to keep on toking

I walk out into tonight, all blustery
You’re going to do something, do it now

Notes of a Pragmatist

The coffee from this morning is not enough to save
Toss it. We'll make more tomorrow. Tonight's dinner
a sort of a beef stroganoff but with chicken

As yet another evening rolls in and says today's over
Set the night for sleeping if you have such power
and throw in a good dream or two just for the fun of it

There's a great desire to float away, be here forever
at least for this brief moment. But all that soon passes
and all time has its insignificant dash of nothingness
The strict understanding of the text makers and the reader

possesses no special powers beyond yes I was there
and this is what I saw. Even the lawyers know the law
remains a construct, open to interpretation by some
others held strictly to precedent and false premises galore

October's Last Monday

News of my brother's impending demise
hard to manage from afar, yet no easier
if I were there. We've been apart too long

All the writers and poets I grew up with are about gone
Most a while ago. I've imbedded what I learned from them
even made proper apologia along the way loving each of them
Their breathed speech tunes my ear as I listen for everyday music

I walk out under the moonless sky as the forecasted rain
begins to fall. Drops dampen my shirt. Nature's tears
replace mine in the time it takes for the dog to wander about
Happy to be living in a diverse neighborhood…not much noise
lots of lights on at night – streetlights, porchlights, nightlights

I used to live like a vampire mining other peoples' dreams
Now by ten, it's close the blinds, lock the doors, and sleep just fine

One Afternoon

The whirr of the blower from the heat pump
the movement of warmer air through the ducts
the background sounds maintaining the balance
in this insulated isolation from natural elements

Water/food still need to be brought in
and wastes brought out and used right

More than enough room for the two of us, a dog
and occasional visitors (when the pandemic dies

The TV news fails to cover the good stuff. I know
very little of what is happening in the rest of the world
I'm quite content with the small part I'm living in

The slope of the backyard, the many trees, the gardens
I keep the birdfeeder filled with nuts, dried berries
sunflower seeds – top of the line for birds migrating

Painters

Lacking a worldview to adhere to
they get lost in the middle of the day

Looking to clean a utensil, a tool
even a small machine, they think
it's good to know where the dirt hides
only works so far as a clear vision

It's not a carrot they need, though
they do like to munch crunchy carrots
No, there are reasons a plenty to go on
— if not out of habit alone…

They see the lack of whatever it is
brushing the canvas with clean brushes

The main plan: keep the process going
See what happens when the ideas arrive

Probably Best

A friend who bordered on the politically conservative
stopped smoking pot and got very critical of America
which he felt it was his right to pipe off, have his say
I saw him as out of touch, unnecessarily self-righteous
I tried to listen to his literary rants. He was a friend

We both think the other doesn't know what he's talking
about, and that may be true. I usually don't dis him
just his views, and only in my own mind. I still like him

He was a drunk, now he's a wine connoisseur
I'm still a pothead who likes a bit of bourbon at night

I used to write about anti-vaxxers and Christian bimbos
who must have been absent a lot from History class

Tired of reading about what's wrong with this country
I've turned my focus to gardening and abstract painting

Quirks

How quickly things whirl out of control
The floor shifts and warps for a second
The chair floats in this room that spins
The falconer takes off her leather glove
Today won't get much above freezing
Patches of black ice wait to terrify

All communications happen online
Pix on the phone fulfill finer than words
To hear another's voice sounds passé
Yet many vote to continue as we were

Selfies of alter egos contain little clues
Old photos darken in years of sunshine

The days go by all on their own
Life says yes or no as it wishes

Ritual

An ache in the bicep upsets sleep
Dreams unravel. Sweat twists the sheets
The night lingers. The slow light of dawn
signals morning, wakens the dog

Feed the beast, make the coffee
Let the dog out, nuke a frozen bagel
two chicken breakfast sausages

Check the weather, pour a cup
Check the headlines, put peanut butter
on that split and toasted bagel

Don't forget the daily meds
Ipad the crossword, Sudoku, and
the Spelling Bee, then solve today's
    picture-puzzle on the can

Standing under the Sky

Oh it was all such a long time ago come back around again
And every song along the way shouted out as if we knew
the notes, the lyrics, what would happen with our lives

Even old folks said they saw the end before it was in sight
A glorious morning that turned into a wonderful night

Anyone looking to sum it all up in a couple of words
misses the point of silence, fails at the art of listening

You can say you want to follow each and every rule
Then you go and break the law just by being you
Forgive those who didn't forgive you, just step away

It's still warm for a night in early December
Funny what we forget, sad what we remember

Count the years and add up all those grand times
'cause this is it. Make room for what ever comes next

Y'All

It's got to have a beat, tempo, or over reaching arches
Elsewise no dancing's going to happen any night this week

Could be a storm or a squeaky violin — there's always music!

I'd rather not the drums of war, not the stilling of the heart
They have their time and pace...just not my bit to play

Break it to yourself — *The Times They Are a-Changin* again
    You might hold out for a higher price
        but you're still selling yourself too cheap

Ply the imagination, take flights of reality, dig into history
turn a phrase, enter a new phase, clock the faces of the moon

Sooner or later you'll be singing a tune, new
or old. Until then stand in your doorway, or go out
under the starry night sky, or walk with some one
else, maybe someone you just met — then y'all sing out

Wednesday Data

A slow rain all day pools in the low spots
A few could use French drains thru the clay

Washed out—how quick a slab can crack, crumble
If I were working the gates of a canal, I too
would clear the debris in the sluices,
let the water flow, the rain falls

Drops barely plopping in the birdbath
so the dog and I head to the mailbox
and back without getting too wet

Easter's based on a pagan holiday in certain latitudes
Persephone returns despite any of our attitudes

Blooms and flowers welcoming the wetness
Hostas poke through the garden soil, grow inches
in but hours. One hopes they survive a late frost

Whitman Stuff

I repeat myself? I have a lot of voices speaking thru me
And they are going to have their say no matter what I say
I don't mind the idea of death; it's the hard truth that hurts
We're all one making believe we are many, that's well known

The universal implications of string theory scare the czars
They pick at their scars as if to find meaning in such pain

Revolution should lead to freedom and equality, not tyranny
The nationalists got to go global in a positive way. End rhyme
remains suspect in the post post-world – is there going to be
chains or moss growing about the remaining bio-clime

Romantic values fail to inspire the masses who only
want to be blessed and nurtured further into a stupor
Rock and Roll might stop delivering escape routes
What happens is beyond us, yet up to us. I repeat myself

Working within Limitations

Took a look at some of the electrical hookups – sub-standard
Time to call in an electrician to get all these wires uncrossed

The wind kicks up, remnant of a nor'easter that roared
thru last night with lightning cracking overhead, thunder
crisp just nano-seconds behind the flash. Almost hit the floor

in response to that raucous clap. Half an hour later
the storm passes, and you and I settle in for the night

A couple now for nearly forty years still striving to finish
our own sentences, never mind each other's thoughts or
the prayers we neither wasted nor cast skyward

All adding up to what, one might ask
Yet we continue as much out of habit as clear thought
turning into pure action – solid stances, good grips
and our ability to suss out the knottiest of problems

Yoga Boots

It’s true, Nature does not know our names
Wind and water care less what we think or feel

A sheet of ice on the roof keeps melting
dripping over the gutters into slush
on the deck best cleared by broom
Popped nail heads would clip a shovel

The high wind gusts come in high
Not much bother to trees by power lines

Meanwhile, the night will dip below freezing
So stay warm, be happy and kind as you can be

Tomorrow tree workers here at 9:30 a.m.
The next day the third attempt at major
upgrading of the house’s electrical system
We’ll see how that all goes. I’ll let you know

Zero Tolerance

The trick, it seems, is to spend less time on social media
Better to lie in bed in the morning and catch dream reruns
That is, if you still want to keep in touch with childhood friends

Important things need be dealt with honesty and humility
These times are ripe for satire yet nothing is gained by it
So best sometimes to cut all ties with pessimistic influences

Most people don't know what they want only what they don't want

Which is fine by me but some prefer to pick a fight
Kicking me even though I left hours ago – thinking they got
my goat – when I don't have a goat, a cow, or chickens, just a dog

I know not what to make of or say to political obsessions

It's best, I've found, to cut off any and all access – block the call
unfriend, and toss any mail from nasty, hurtful people who want
me to play cop in their overly dramatic death-by-cop scenarios

March 6th Again

A slow steady rain coming down on a day
when a fifty-six year old memory haunts
the back of my mind, back when I thought
this living meant something and the hard words
my brother spoke were the last words he said
but I didn't know that then a mere seventeen

The rain total is going be less than forecast
Fine by me. I'm done researching the past

The scars on my chest start itching at this hour
then stop as if listening to my thoughts

Waiting for the world to stop going crazy
Hard to take the old mind games too seriously

Better to forget those loves that almost lasted
than attempt to reconcile the past with now

Revision

Perhaps I've been living in the woods too long
away from society and its people
Decorum has its purpose and it is sorely missed

but not by the vicious minority. The times changed
a while ago – many a daylight savings since then
The petty arguments mere distractions while corpora-
tions seek to liquidate everybody's bank account

Yeah, let's go hobnob with the folks on the North Neck
A mid-September day sampling oysters and wines
may be just what I need to feel a bit more human

Less than a ten-dollar bottle of Cabernet Sauvignon
works fine sitting on the back porch in this forest

Here's to freedom! Here's to equality!
Next the justice needed to get us there

Plink, Pluck, Plunk

Most days I'm happy when the world leaves me alone
though I'm sure its wrong doings will affect me soon
I do hope I can handle doing what's right then
Even if it's the toughest thing to do
I hope I don't whimper about what I could've done
    to make that doing much easier

But I've known people who went back on their ways
who sought some mercy in their final days – comfort
    Truly, it's a hard thing to measure

I've no reason to judge them, I'm neither a judge nor
a lawyer. I have studied Rhetoric and Composition
and if I remember even a bit of it I can tell when
some one is trying to pull wool over my eyes, as well
the sounds wooden nickels make hitting the ground

Red Moon

Spring falters mid-April with a cold morning
and a sheet of snow turned to ice covers
what was beginning to sprout after the crocus
came and went. The hyacinth wilts, stunted

Yet by noon the sun warms the ground
no further cause for alarm. The cold stays
but it's above freezing! I'm back toting seed
trays back and forth from a day's sunshine
to night time warmth on kitchen counters

When things occur like the moon turning red
I look for the effects upon the earth, my own small
plot of land in this place I've lived for some time

Some force tripped up. Now Spring's a gazelle
leaping long-legged – it leaps amazingly well

We Might've Thought Spring Springs Eternal

I want to tell you that spring will come
surely different with its blooming
than those we once danced about giddy
tripping about the flowers and sunshine

We too were returning from Hades
set loose from the darkness of our youths
Spring enlivened our souls and bodies

Proof seems to indicate that wind and rain
will be too much for growing flowers
trees will fall, river banks will overflow

There're too many of us, not enough
higher ground for all to stand upon
Gonna be interesting as that curse states
who helps whom, how that works, who lives on

Between

I feel something but it doesn't last long
And that's okay 'cause I got enough
going on to keep busy without losing
focus and forgetting what I'm doing

All I have now is what I can do
Falling asleep in the middle of the day
while white clouds mackerel a blue sky

Not waiting for salvation
Not wasting forgiveness
Not willing to beg for mercy
Not wishing for love any less

I relax myself listening as old songs
play variations on love and death
Trying to tell the difference

Growing Up

It took me a while to figure out how to not end up
puking and passing out. I preferred to vomit outside
It seemed more natural. But sometimes I'd get sick
inside and once in someone's bedroom: alcohol
food chunks, bile all over their bed covers

I know who it was who cleaned my mess up
You're the last I apologize to. Thank you!

I knew so little about you – you were a shadow
another making one's way in a chaotic world
May you have that good life you worked hard for

"I'd have a cocktail," you'd say, "never more than two
and if there were a good dinner, some great wine too"

But it's edibles we prefer all these days since
hearing meaning fade like a lilting tune in the air

After A Good Night's Sleep

Breakfast and coffee lead me to the crossword puzzle
which only takes a few moments to complete, then
Sudoku and the Spelling Bee – another nine or so
I soon feel like I should get dressed and do something

Perhaps something that benefits others – but I'm stuck
cleaning up my own mess first, and that's taken years

Morning rain and early afternoon sunshine stays chilly
I leash the dog to get the mail, mostly junk. The dog and I
mosey about the front yard watching out for holes where
bushes had been dug up – no need to twist an ankle
or take a fall. Instead, I wonder what plants I could set
to add bright colors to the landscape. Of course, they'd
need to be deer-resistant. No bulbs for squirrels to eat

Eden had no fences, only that stupid rule about knowledge

www.ingramcontent.com/pod-product-compliance
Ingram Content Group UK Ltd.
Pitfield, Milton Keynes, MK11 3LW, UK
UKHW041316190726
13845UKWH00025B/310

9 789363 544321